About Bipolar
"Complete!"
Enemies All Around Me
Episode CI – The Truth about Bigfoot
High on Life
Hillbilly Wedding
In My Apartment
Listen To Kurt Cobain (Acrostic)
Optimistic
Real Good Country Girl
Shopping At the Goodwill Store
Soak Life In
Someone Else
That Country Scene
The Best Part of my Childhood
The Best Possible
The Knockout
Complete I – Discontent
Complete II – Dawn
Complete III – Satisfaction
Green I – The Farm
Insanity I – The Diagnosis
Insanity II – The Fall
Litter I – Declaration
Litter II – War and Peace
Litter III – The Aftermath
Litter IV – A Change on the Plot
Litter V – Funk
New Madrid I – The First
New Madrid II – Survival
Someone Else I – Character Development
Someone Else II – Geriatric
The Social Problem Death

About Bipolar

Though I'm crazy I can't be humble,
I think I'm better that other people,
Since I'm crazy I can drive drunk,
And just for me the DJ plays punk,
I write songs and I never work,
Even celebrities call me a jerk,
I get all this and there's no doubt,
They even put a satellite over my house

Yeah, the girls think that I'm so crazy,
Yeah, the fellas they really hate me,
Yeah, I have the right to be lazy,
In 1999 the whole world did date me

Since I'm crazy the best write songs about me,
Ball games would've turned out different without me,
Though I'm crazy, I'm not actually crazy,
Yeah, that satellite really came to save me,
Pretty girls were sent to make me better,
I think I even affected the weather,
I have connections the whole world about,
And they even placed a satellite over my house

Yeah, this has never been done,
Yeah, I am the One,
Yeah, I'm known throughout the nations,
And you thought you had hallucinations.

"Complete!"

I'm going to write a book and call it "Complete!"
And then live it out for all the world to see,
I'll return to college,
But not just for knowledge,
I'll exercise at night and write movies,
I'm going to live life right and live life groovy!

Live my life with no regrets!
A celebrity and better, yet!
Live my life with no regrets!

I'll be a collegiate athlete and be great at it,
Win Grammies and Oscars with my wit,
And I'll still stay quite spiritual in front of the world,
And I'll marry me a good girl!
Because I want the world to see me,
Live out the book "Complete!"!

Live my life with no regrets!
Rich and famous and better, yet!
Live my life with no regrets!

"Enemies All Around Me"

Blame it all on the dope
I'm a man with no hope
And I look so evil in the mirror
What once was so gorgeous
Is now just a feign before us
To make this lonely view clearer
I saw the surprise
And the shock in their eyes
When I showed up high for 8 months
As my scenes get scary
And my safety can vary
I always hate that I just live once

And I got enemies all around me
So damn lucky that the cops haven't found me
And I use meth
With the people I'm with
They don't know much about social graces
But intoxication is my oasis
So I got enemies all around me

Well, I don't have a clue
If it's the drugs or the flu
When I get sick to my stomach
I'm far too stupid to care
As I drive stoned everywhere
Not seeing the stupidity of it
Then like a fool
I flunk out of school
I'd spent my study time hunting drugs
I would show more resistance
And improve my existence
But I'm surrounded by no one but thugs

And I got enemies all around me
So damn lucky that the cops haven't found me
And I use meth
With the people I'm with
They don't know much about social graces
But intoxication is my oasis
So I got enemies all around me

Episode CI

The Truth about Bigfoot

A long, long time ago in a galaxy far, far away, the entire galaxy had grown extremely unsafe because of thousands of years of pollution. The drones were growing powerful since they didn't have to breathe the air. They had gained nearly all control of the gas mask and resistant armor black market.

The Jedi-trained Wookie, Smackghum, had put in motion a plan to save his race from extinction. He used Jedi mind tricks to make the scientific creators of the clones build a vessel that could extend outside of the galaxy.

As the galaxy faced its destruction, the two dark sith lords, Gizmo and Fruto, and their remaining Ewok relatives, rushed to gain this new technology. Cunningly, after Smackgum had made sure only one vessel was created, he murdered all the creative scientists. Then he sent about 10 Wookies safely toward a spiral galaxy, called The Milky Way.

The Wookie ship would make it safely and find a habitable planet in a solar system located near the edge of the galaxy. The Wookies remained hidden in the less civilized areas of this planet, Earth, for centuries. But now they had found that their existence had been discovered by the human race, who called them by the terms of Sasquatch and Bigfoot….

"High on Life"

I'm really high on life today, there's a smile on my face,
Why must I die and have to leave this place?
Everyone knows how I think it's so good to be existing,
And that it's my immortality that I'm always persisting,

Have you ever just been high on life?
Have you ever just looked around with your eyes and just been high on life?

It's not even possible that we exist!
I would spend an eternity even in this!
So, please, let's all work together in peace,
Because I want my scenes to never cease!

Have you ever just been high on life?
Have you ever just looked around with your eyes and just been high on life?

"Hillbilly Wedding"

There's going to be a hillbilly wedding in June,
And it won't be too soon,
Because she's already pregnant

There's going to be a newborn baby late fall,
And it won't suffer at all,
Because of government assistance

There's going to be substance abuse by a mother,
And her significant other,
Because people are stupid

There's going to be a teenage shoplifter,
And it'll never stop there,
Because they're already ruined

There's going to be a hillbilly wedding in June

"In My Apartment"

I don't play my guitars but they make a great decoration
Though I'm out of shape my bicycle looks good in its station
I clean it nicely for my monthly inspection
I have pictures of friends and family for whom I have affection
Yeah, in my apartment I sometimes dream of the good life
In my apartment I still haven't met my dear wife
Yeah, in my apartment I sure like to unwind
In my apartment I pass on through time!

I cut off my cable for more time and for more money
I'll step outside for a nice walk if the weather is sunny
I may have some beer but I only drink a couple
I no longer run around and get myself in legal trouble
Yeah, in my apartment I'll read The Bible
In my apartment I'll prep to go out in style
Yeah, in my apartment I really have a great time
In my apartment I pass on through life!

Yeah, I'll stay here and pass up richness and fame
And, I'll stay here and have a small town good name
I'll stay here as the time has come and it has went
Yeah, I'll stay in my apartment and try to be content.

"Listen To Kurt Cobain (Acrostic)"

Lazy we were in a time of bad behavior
In support with loyalty to our savior
So far from what we should have done
Taking in everything including the sun
Every night another wild adventure to live
Not understanding our future we would give
Thoughts were impressed into our good times
Obsessed we were with Kurt Cobain's rhymes
Knowledge of the bad at an age too young
United to wear the songs he'd sung
Runaways and thugs is what we were called
The dangerous underground is where we crawled
Common knowledge of us spread the scenes
Overcoming preppy reps to be known as feigns
By time 16 we were accomplished thieves
Amazing people with our amount of heaves
I'd end up turning into a well mannered adult
Never forgetting, though, that ole Nirvana cult

"Optimistic"

I'm the dishwasher,
I'm that crazy dishwasher,
I'm that angry dishwasher,
And I'm still alive
Yeah, I'm the dishwasher,
I'm that crazy dishwasher,
I'm that angry dishwasher,
And I'm still alive

I'm optimistic for my brainwaves
I'm optimistic to have a continual feast
I'm optimistic to beat depression
I'm optimistic so I can be a beast

I'm the dishwasher,
I'm that crazy dishwasher,
I'm that angry dishwasher,
And I'm still alive
Yeah, I'm the dishwasher,
I'm that crazy dishwasher,
I'm that angry dishwasher,
And I'm still alive

I'm optimistic like an affirmation
I'm optimistic that there's an afterlife
I'm optimistic and I'm grinning
Since I'm optimistic I've beat suicide

I'm the dishwasher,
I'm that crazy dishwasher,
I'm that angry dishwasher,
And I'm still alive
Yeah, I'm the dishwasher,
I'm that crazy dishwasher,
I'm that angry dishwasher,
And I'm still alive

"Real Good Country Girl"

I want a real good country girl
I want a real good country girl

She'll be moral and chaste
With a pretty little face
Wearing ribbons and curls
In our beautiful world

I want a real good country girl
I want a real good country girl

She'll be the happy type
With a twinkle in her eye
Faithful and true
Yeah, she'll never be cruel

I want a real good country girl
I want a real good country girl

Yeah, she'll be so good looking
Making that tasty home cooking
And I'll have a lifetime of
Having someone so awesome to love

I want a real good country girl
I want a real good country girl

"Shopping at the Goodwill Store"

People look down on me
Because of my reality
But still I dress pretty nice
In clothes that do suffice
I get my jeans from Wal-Mart
Nice stores have clearances that are smart
I hit myself a garage or two
But there's some thing else to do

Shopping at the Goodwill Store
Shopping at the Goodwill Store
Yeah, your dollar always gets you more
Shopping at the Goodwill Store

I was raised to keep my belt tight
And to spend my money right
Talk the price down if I can
Buy from a need-to-sale man
A dollar saved is a dollar earned
To get a bargain I've learned
And one thing is for sure
Your dollar will always get you more

Shopping at the Goodwill Store
Shopping at the Goodwill Store
Yeah, your dollar always gets you more
Shopping at the Goodwill Store

A nice jersey less ten bucks
The same for a shirt with French cuffs
Shoes originally a hundred plus
Yeah, you can get so much stuff

Shopping at the Goodwill Store
Shopping at the Goodwill Store
Yeah, your dollar always gets you more
Shopping at the Goodwill Store
Yeah, shopping at the Goodwill Store

"Soak Life In"

Soak Life In, Look Around Again…

Step outside on a starry night,
Sober as can be and that's alright,
Think about the blessing of our grand existence,
And soak life in with a little persistence!

Soak Life In, Look Around Again…

Lie down at night and just close your eyes,
And think about life itself deep down inside,
You just see black but you feel so much more,
And despite your problems you want to wake up for sure!

Soak Life In, Look Around Again…

Sit down on a muddy bank and think, "This is nice,
I'm going to spend this day in a paradise,"
Sit and pray, sit and meditate,
Yeah, it's times like these that life's so great!

Soak Life In, Look Around Again…

"Someone Else"

Well, I woke up as someone else,
I made it to a mirror just to see myself,
I was old and dying,
Man, I started crying!

I'd always wanted to fix this world,
But now in a must situation I was hurled,
Because I woke up old and dying,
So I started trying!

I called my congressman and I said, "Hi,
Tell the President that I don't want to die.
Give me 'Peace and Security',
So science can concentrate on saving me!"

I'd always wanted to be rich and famous,
But now the situation was a must,
Because I was old and dying,
So I kept on trying!

I called an agent and I said, "Hey,
Make me famous so that I can say,
'Give me 'Peace and Security',
So science can concentrate on saving me!"

"Give me 'Peace and Security',
So science can concentrate on saving me!"

"That Country Scene"

I was raised on my grandfather's farm,
There's never been a greater man,
I was taught to be kind and warm,
And to do good deeds whenever I can,
Popcorn and "Hee-Haw" on a Saturday night,
There was even a sorghum mill there,
I grew to treat people right,
And I grew to truly care,
The love I was shown on that country scene,
Means as much to me as anything.

I'd return to that farm,
After spending junior high away,
I caused nothing but harm,
To those still alive that day,
Nirvana posters hung 6 miles from town,
That's where I stumbled home to each night,
And as I angered everyone around,
Mom and Grandma still loved me right,
And that love I was shown on that country scene,
Means as much to me as anything.

I would still be on that farm at the age 21,
I'd totally torn my world apart,
But quite a change in me had truly begun,
As my dear grandmother reached my heart,
It would be after she died that I finally got sober,
But now it's been over ten years clean,
But I still I wish I could live my life over,
For the dear ones I've hurt in my family,
That love I knew on that country scene,
Still means more to me then anything.

"The Best Part of my Childhood"

We'd dig up grub worms from under some hay,
Through the field we'd be on our way,
It was 1988
Grandpa's land had three ponds,
We had strong family bonds,
Yeah, life was great!

We'll catch 50 perch today,
Or some catfish we may,
While Grandma's cooking dinner
We're not some doctor's sons,
But they're not the only ones,
Who feel like a winner!

Dear to my heart,
I had a nice start,
To this life that we're living
If I could see them today,
The first things I'd say,
Would be, "I love you, and thanks for all of your giving."

We'll catch 50 perch today,
Or some catfish we may,
While Grandma's cooking dinner
We're not some lawyer's sons,
But they're not the only ones,
Who feel like a winner!

I had a nice start,
To this life we're living!

"The Best Possible"

I had the best mother I could have ever had!

She was strong after the death of dad,
She was strong after the death of dad,
I had the best mother I could have ever had!

She was the single mother that could do no bad,
She was the single mother that could do no bad,
I had the best mother I could have ever had!

She sacrificed so that I was the teenage fad,
She sacrificed so that I was the teenage fad,
I had the best mother I could have ever had!

She was there for me when I got sad,
She was there for me when I got sad,
I had the best mother I could have ever had!

When they treat her wrong I get mad,
When they treat her wrong I get mad,
I had the best mother I could have ever had!

Her son's the happiest to be alive…

"The Knockout"

She's what you call a knockout,
What I want my life about,
She pulls off wearing spandex,
And makes my life so complex,
Myself, I get obsessive,
And force the fact that we're in love,
Then pretty soon I found out,
What it means to be a knockout!

She's what you call a knockout,
Her scenes are known all about,
And I'm going crazy,
As I think she's going to save me,
Myself, I act psychotic,
As the only one who ever saw it,
Then *I became a college dropout,*
Because there's what you call a knockout!

She's what you call a knockout,
In her eyes I'm not about,
She was so far above me,
How dare I think that she should love me,
And myself, I'm quite pathetic,
Those foolish acts I can't forget,
And I still live my life without,
What you call a knockout!

Complete I

Discontent

Chicago Spencer turned 34 years old today. He had been rather content lately, but that wasn't the norm. Usually, Chicago daydreamed of fame and fortune. He did this much more than most other people. However, this birthday had made him even more unstable.

But what would Chicago do? He doesn't know how to act. He can't play any musical instruments. He's not in great physical condition. Honestly, he's quite out of shape. He's not even able to work because he's currently on disability due to mental health reasons! How would he afford medicine without being eligible for government assistance? Could he do anything at all?

But on the other hand, what could Chicago do? He's very discontent and extremely creative. He quit college early in his sophomore year. That would give him three years of athletic qualification. So he could be a collegiate athlete! He hadn't smoked tobacco or used drugs in over a decade, besides just a handful of mistakes. Though he'd never played competitive sports, he had *quite* a lot of knowledge about athletics. He watched sports several hours a day, if he watched anything.

Chicago had also written lyrics for many, many years due to his unstable behavior. In fact, he'd made a demo album with the help of a friend that he has that knows how to create electronic music on computers. The album wasn't in correct musical timing, due to Chicago's lack of intelligence about music. However, it still was an *awesome album*! It had *world class* lyrics! It was a *generational*, if not an *all-time* creation!

Chicago also had several nice ideas for movies. These ran from the film World War III, to a film about a man who magically awoke as an old man one day. *What would he do now facing his mortality?* There were others, too. He didn't speak of them to most people for fear of having his ideas stolen.

Chicago wanted to do it all! He wanted to be an athlete, a musician, and a film star! If anyone could pull this off, it was Chicago Spencer.

It was currently late July. Chicago decided to spend the next five months getting into world class physical shape. He'd also planned on writing a couple of his movie ideas. Finally, he was going to get an album radio ready by the year's end.

Chicago truly treasured his existence. He wanted to be living the best life that he possibly could.

He didn't even know for sure if anybody else was truly alive. Could everyone else just be weird things for him in his life? Was life about a choice to make- *either live life to the fullest or be religious?* He wondered if he could do both? What was he suppose to do with this miraculous existence?

Honestly, Chicago really didn't know the answers to those questions. However, he didn't want to waste anymore of his life!

Yes, Chicago was finally choosing to really live his life to the full! And, what's more, he still wanted to be a good person.

So Chicago sat down that day and spent hours and hours working on his first major project. He was writing a story titled "Complete!" It was very interesting. In "Complete!" a young man writes a work named "Complete!" Then the character lives out the story in real life, which takes him through a public view of sports, fame, and fortune.

Yes, in front of the world, *he would complete* "Complete!"

Complete II

Dawn

Now, Chicago was not a morning person, at all. But, once again, *he had decided* to drastically change his life. He wanted to break his routine of sleeping in and then not accomplishing anything with his day. He began by promptly getting out of bed at 4:00 a.m.

He had made a schedule for the day. But he had made a schedule for the day many, many times. He'd last two days at the most. And usually he lasted less than a minute. He'd just turn off his alarm clock and go back to bed. He always wanted to stay awake and stick to a day's plan. But he just couldn't stay awake and/or work. He prayed that today he would finally succeed! He prayed he would finally keep a schedule! But he always prayed like that when morning came.

Chicago ate some milk and cereal. Then he used a yoga video that was part of complete exercise video system he'd bought. He really enjoyed the stretches. They were relaxing and he knew it would help his muscles grow. He always had the videos around. And he always was intent on using them. But he never used them. He was very happy that he did today.

Afterwards, Chicago walked through town to its main fitness center. Weightlifting,, he worked his legs out this morning. He worked out intensely. He was always intent on *using the gym membership* for what it was costing him financially. He certainly used it today. He just considered it a beginning of great things to come.

After Chicago made it back to his apartment he showered. Then he shaved real careful and diligent. He brushed his teeth for ten minutes, using a lot of whitening toothpaste.

After getting cleaned up, Chicago practiced guitar for a couple hours. He always had guitars around. He always intended to use them, but they just gathered dust. He practiced for a good amount of time today. *He did what he should have always been doing.*

Chicago dug out an old Intermediate College Algebra book he'd saved. He read over the first chapter's lessons and then he did the exercises. He made an 88% when he checked the answers in the back of the book. Not only did he want to finish college, Chicago really wanted to have great mathematical knowledge. He learned just a little today. It was a nice start. His target to return to college was still five months away.

At last, Chicago got started working on the first film he desired to write - "Complete!" He'd spent years longing to put to use all his music and film ideas. He'd always just given up on his dreams, simply throwing away his work shortly after starting. But he really, really wanted to create his visions! *He wanted tangible success!* Today he kept writing!

Chicago made a detail cleaning of his apartment that evening. He was proud of it.

So Chicago Spencer had worked vigorously from 4:00 in the morning until 8:00 in the evening. He had not wasted a minute. He had not given in to fears and doubts. He had even eaten healthy.

A college athlete moonlighting as a music and film maker! That was Chicago's mission!

He had "completed" quite a day!

Complete III

Satisfaction

Chicago Spencer had worked hard for five long months. *He had studied math to help him with his return to college. Even though he was already 34 years old, he had trained himself into world class physical condition. He had learned a lot about playing guitar. Chicago even finished his first two quality screenplays.*

Now it was January. School had arrived!

After taking 4 classes from 8:00 to 12:00 that morning, Chicago wasted no time. He bravely made his way to the athletic facilities. He'd spent half of a year getting ready for this moment.

He was stopped by a security guard.

"This is a restricted area."

"I'm sorry, sir. Can you tell me how you try to walk-on to the teams here?" Chicago bravely spoke up.

"Wait here." the security guard commanded. "I'll see if anybody can help you today."

"Thank you so much, sir." Chicago replied.

After a few minutes the guard returned with two men. They were both assistant coaches.

"How can we help you?" one of the coaches asked.

"I want to play college sports." Chicago courageously stated.

"Where did you play high school ball?" one said.

"Honestly, I've never been on an organized team, Coach. But I've played more pick up games than anyone you know, I've played many sports video games, and I watch sports on television *addictively*. And I've been physically training six months for this."

"We can't use you if you don't already have experience in organized ball. Playing video games doesn't make you know enough to walk on to a collegiate team."

"*I can bench press 375 pounds and run a four minute mile.*" Chicago tried reasoning, "*I'm probably in better shape than your players.*"

"Sorry, kid. It takes more than physical ability." They told him.

"Please, sir." He begged. "*I'll guarantee you I'll lead you to national titles.* I'll learn fast. I can start as a pinch runner or a defensive intensity guy.

"I'm sorry." They told him as they turned and went away.

Chicago was overcome with emotion. He was really hurt. Five months of diet, yoga and exercise *for nothing*. Heartbroken, Chicago made his way to the campus cafeteria to eat lunch. He was extremely upset and discouraged.

As Chicago was eating his lunch, pondering his life, his cell phone rang.

"Hello."

"Is this Chicago Spencer?" asked the lady on the phone.

"Yeah, this is him.", trying to be nice while angry.

"How are you doing, Mr. Spencer?

"Oh, it's good to be alive!" He replied as usual does in his pleasantries.

"No argument here. I've got some good news for you, Chicago." She said.

"You do?" He wondered.

"Yes, I do. My name is Bea Goode. I'm a talent agent. I really liked the screenplays you sent me, *and your demo album, too!*"

Green I

The Farm

They lived an old-fashioned life style in rural Oklahoma during the late 1980's.

John McCartney was just 8 years old and *green* to the world. He woke up in the guestroom at his grandparent's house. He was refreshed. It was a nice place to sleep. The window unit air conditioner had done its job. On vacation mode, it had just cut off before he woke up. John was nice, comfortable and cool.

His little feet hit the carpet floor. They made it quickly into the kitchen two rooms away.

"Is that John?" his grandfather playfully asked with a smile. "Is that John?"

He couldn't help but smile back. Then he ran across the room and gave his grandfather a hug around the knees.

"Are we going fishing today?" he asked.

"We can. But work is first. After the garden, I might let you and your brother work on the new shed with me, *if you want*?" His grandfather grinned.

"Cool, Grandpa! Thanks!"

They said a prayer and then they ate breakfast. The telephone rang. Grandma talked while John and Grandpa finished eating.

After she hung up she said, "Your brother is walking up the lane. Go get your rubber boots on. We need to get started."

The four of them walked through the small orchard on the way to the bigger of the two gardens on the land. There wasn't any fruit, yet, but the trees were beginning to show spring buds and flowers.

The large vegetable plot was always very well prepared. Grandpa had plowed it with a disc behind his tractor and then even turned it over again with a large tiller. The boys were making fast progress putting seed down and covering up their holes. Grandpa and Grandma couldn't bend over and work like them. So they used an idea they'd had. They dropped the seeds down a four foot plastic pipe, right into the hole.

It was hard work. But that was the norm. They'd worked hard their entire life. They wanted to live off the land.

After leaving the garden, Grandpa had the boys help with the new shed. All they really did was help mix gravel and concrete to make the floor. Grandpa had a lot of life experience, including carpentry skills.

About 10:30 he told the boys, "Let's go down to the pond!"

Excited, they put their tools and tool-belts up. Then they ran to a special barrel filled with dirt with hay on the top of it. They removed the hay. Then they grabbed some of the earthworms from inside the barrel and put them in a couple of old tin coffee cans.

They rode in an old, blue Ford farm truck, through a road in the pasture passing by cattle.

The boys were catching and releasing little perch by the minute. When they ran out of worms Grandpa, told them to catch some grasshoppers from the field. *It was just perfect happiness for all of them.*

"Lunch is probably ready, boys."

Back at the house, they all ate dinner as they listened to Paul Harvey on the radio, giving the country the news. They played checkers and dominoes for a while.

Then Uncle Tom, their son, came in the front door.

"Wow, do I have a story for you guys." He said. "We took the boat down to the river to check the trotlines. We were just trolling around, enjoying ourselves, checking the lines.

We saw a large tree that had kind of fallen away from the bank. All you could really see of it was the roots. And there was a moccasin on top of the dirt pile.

We'd brought the pistol with us. So like morons we shot at it. 15 snakes came out of holes in that root system that we hadn't noticed! It was crazy! If you leaned away from the snakes on one side, the person on the other side of the boat would almost have water, if not snakes, coming in on his side of the boat. It was unbelievable!

That trolling motor was never slower! We kept the snakes at bay and we finally got out of there. We did get a few nice catfish, though." He joked.

The boys would spend the late afternoon, after naps, watching cartoons. Then they went back to their house, down the lane, once their mother got home from work. They'd eat dinner with that special young widowed mother. Then they all watched television on the couch together, until their 8:00 bedtime.

Insanity I

The Diagnosis

The story begins 15 years ago, as young David Jones was throwing a fit in his bedroom. He threw over his desk. He yelled and cursed. He even threatened to commit suicide.

The sheriff deputy made his way out to the home, which was out in the country. The deputy placed David in handcuffs, and they headed to a mental hospital an hour and a half away. During the trip the radio in the vehicle played "It's the end of the world as we know it!" by REM. *David thought that the station knew what was going on. And he thought they played the song especially for him.*

After they made it to the hospital, David was placed before the main doctor of the institution. She began to ask him questions.

"What's been going on in your life to make you want to kill yourself?"

He responded, "I'm just really stressed out."

David went on and told her about the little small town conspiracy he was in, and how it was getting bigger.

She then asked him, "Do you have a family history of mental illness?"

He then told her about one of his cousins. His cousin had had full-fledged bipolar disorder during the mid 1990's, before anyone really heard much about the condition.

She told him, "David, you have bipolar disorder."

David didn't know how to react. This was a special change in his life. Wow!

David spent that night in a room that was 100% empty, except for a hospital bed. He was strapped down both by his feet and by his arms.

David was given a choice to go home after three days of lockup or voluntarily stay for three additional weeks.

David told them he'd only stay the three days. He was a community college student and he couldn't miss school or work, for three weeks.

David spent the next day in a mental hospital for the first time. The hard part about being locked up was no ability to work at his life. He was losing time that he could have been using to make money, or otherwise be improving his life.

Even in the hospital, David was actually getting worse. *He watched a football game on the male wing's television and it happened again. This time he thought that the announcers knew who he was, and what was going on.*

David was frightened about his future. Frightened! The three days passed.

He was now a mental health patient!

Insanity II

The Fall

David Jones, just 19, was fresh out of a three day mental hospital stay. He had become unclear as to what was sane and what wasn't.

Sophomore David had chosen to take 6 college courses that fall semester. That was simply too many. He also had to work part-time. He had care for his place of living. David also enjoyed working out. David was truly taking on way too much.

To make matters worse, David really was having severe mental health problems. *He was involved in a nationwide conspiracy*, in his head. It really had begun to affect his performance at any tasks he had to work at.

David had to make some hard decisions. He told the college that he needed to take the semester off to address his mental health. He had been struggling with his grades due to taking on so many classes, anyways.

David's well being was in jeopardy. *He thought that the celebrities of the world had heard about him, because of how interesting his life had become. And they were going to help him out!*

So they had special satellites moved to follow him at all times. They placed hidden cameras at his house, at work, and even in his car. When he watched television, the studio had a satellite feed to where they could see him as they spoke. Everything was live. This went for all radio and television activity. Songs were meant for him with coded messages. Movies subtly had his influence.

The people of fame were there to help David with his life. But most of the time, this delusion was quite mean to him. And as he got more and more disabled, it got worse. It was a miserable experience. It was a*n* extremely miserable experience.

David found a job at a local fish buffet as a dishwasher. David would often leave work after just an hour. He never got fired, though. His boss could tell the painful ordeal he was really going through.

His inability to work caused him to drive a junky car. His role of dishwasher was a true hell which he couldn't overcome. He had the least power at his place of employment. He was covered with water, and he was nasty, by shift's end. He was handicapped mentally, acting like a crazy fool in the place, and everywhere else..

David Jones had become the most depressed person on the planet. He had gone mad! And there was no end in sight.

David's greatest fear was that this intense type of mental health anguish could curse him for the rest of his life!

Litter I

Declaration

"This is about the catfight," The old yellow tomcat said.

"Let's keep it about the catfight, then!" The black and white bobbed-tail young tomcat responded. And he meant about the catfight that was *about* to happen.

The old yellow tomcat was named Syracuse and the young tomcat was called Oreo. They were fighting about an earlier catfight between Oreo and a female cat named Georgette.

They boys began growling and hissing at one another. Each one was very nervous, angry, and quite cautious. The instant that old yellow cat leaped, so did the young one. They met head on at the same time. They rolled around wrestling in a big ball of anger. Then they separated at the same time. They hissed and growled, again. Then they lunged at each other again. They rolled around fighting, again. However, after this time when they stopped wrestling the young bobbed-tail cat took off running away.

Syracuse wasted no time in pursuing his young opponent.

Oreo made a quick run up a tree. When he was just a couple of feet up the tree Syracuse leaped up knocking Oreo back down on the ground. This time they clawed each other extremely violently. Young Oreo even got a deep bite into Syracuse, nearly taking the right ear off of his older adversary.

Syracuse quickly retreated fleeing off the entire country farm into the woods. Oreo gave up the chase as Syracuse went into the higher grass and thicker brush.

As Syracuse stood there by himself in the woods paranoid about his safety still, he began to pity himself. He'd lived in this area for over a decade. He had many children and grandchildren. The widowed farmer's wife who owned the land still had loved him for many, many years. He remembered the love of her petting and the joy of their playing. Georgette was his favorite mate that he'd ever had. He knew the battle wasn't over. He'd been around a long time and fought through many wars.

Meanwhile, Oreo climbed up into the old gray barn. He placed himself in a position to see Syracuse if he decided to return to the farm. Oreo suddenly realized that in the fight he'd hurt his front right foot. He didn't notice the pain until the adrenaline of the fight stopped. He could tell that he would be limping for a couple of days.

For the remainder of the day and through the night Oreo stayed up in the safety of the barn. He had climbed his way to the very top of the square hay bales stacked deep into the building. He rested nice, warm and comfortable.

However, Syracuse had it much harder. He hardly slept that night. It was raining and cold. He only found shelter below a small tree that had fallen over. He curled up below it the best he could to stay warm and dry. But it was a miserable night. He kept half awake for fear of predators.

Past midway through the night, Syracuse heard the coyotes barking. He spent the rest of the morning on the lookout.

As the rain fell and the coyotes yelled, Oreo couldn't help but to smile. And it was almost an evil grin. It wasn't completely, though. Deep inside Oreo felt sorry for Syracuse that night. He respected his old foe.

Morning finally came for the farm. No one knew what would happen next?

Litter II

War and Peace

That old and yellow cat Syracuse headed back to the farm with his bitten ear and his lack of rest from the miserable, unsheltered night.

Young Oreo, with only his hurt foot from their fight, was able to sleep in nicely. He had spent that night comfortable on the squared hay that was stacked high in that well-built barn.

Syracuse went out of his way and circled to the north side of the farm's yard for his entrance. He was hoping to not be seen by Oreo. He cautiously slithered under a barbwire fence and entered the yard. He crouched lowly as he approached slowly.

Things changed suddenly!

Near the back porch of the house Syracuse saw a small copperhead. He was in no mood to kill a snake today. He was tired from his terrible night. He knew his duty, though.

He'd killed several small snakes before, but he was still careful. He crept up on the snake. He rose up on his back feet and put his front arm out to grab the snake. Suddenly the house door opened!

The old lady of the house walked straight to the shed and grabbed a garden hoe. She came back and cut the snake's head off with one swing. She reached down and petted Syracuse and praised him for his love and bravery. She would have never noticed the snake was there without Syracuse.

The lady then called all the cats to come up to be fed. Both Syracuse and Oreo came slowly, wary of each other. The two tomcats growled as they ate next to each other. The woman scolded them both when she saw their wounds.

The two tomcats looked at each other face to face. Then they turned away and left. Then for three days they had an unspoken truce. They only did this so that their own wounds could heal.

Oreo stayed safe up in the barn. Old Syracuse slept on top of a car underneath the carport connected to the home. He was still very cold at night. But he was glad to be out of the rain and much safer from predators now.

Each day they just stared and growled at the other one during feeding time, with an occasional hiss. They had nothing to say to the other. They were both extremely careful to not make any sudden movements that might react with a fight.

Old Syracuse had been here before. He'd fought many wars against many other cats in the past. He'd been a tomcat in this rural area for a long time. He figured it wasn't over yet.

Young Oreo wasn't nearly as experienced. He didn't know what would happen. He just told himself he'd fight as hard and long as possible. He feared Syracuse's life experience.

It had been three days since their fight. After breakfast that morning, Syracuse was distracted as he turned to leave. He'd let his guard down! While he was blind to Oreo behind him, Oreo immediately jumped on Syracuse's back. He landed directly on top of Syracuse, clawing him and then biting his head.

Syracuse managed to flip Oreo forward over him. The two cats turned into a ball of war, rolling around violently. Syracuse got free and fled. This time *he* went into the barn. Oreo knew he shouldn't give up that nice, warm barn that he loved to sleep in at night. So Oreo chased Syracuse to the top of the stack of hay. He lunged at Syracuse.

Syracuse managed to duck under the attack. Oreo overshot and went through the upper window of the building. He fell 15 feet onto the ground outside.

Oreo was seriously hurt.

Litter III

The Aftermath

Oreo tried making his way back to the house of the farm. Though young and strong, he still couldn't walk on his front left leg. His black and white fur was covered with dirt and grass. He had a little blood on his face. He kept yelling with his loudest meow. The lady of the farm heard him and went looking for him.

She picked up and gave him an encouraging hug. She brought him into the house. She dug out her pet caddy to put him in to transfer him to the vet. They came out of the house and got into her old red Chevrolet pickup. They headed to town.

Old Syracuse had kept his distance. He watched the house from on top of the tin roof of the little tool shed that was on the property. He was visibly upset. For four days now he'd been at war with Oreo. And he felt justified for his anger. Oreo had hurt Georgette. Georgette was a female. But this war had gotten out of hand. And he'd been in wars that had gotten out of hand before.

Oreo relaxed and rested up on his trip to town. The vet took him back to his examining room. The x-rays showed a complete fracture in the top half of Oreo's leg. The vet said he'd knock Oreo out, set the bone, and put a stint on him. He would need to stay overnight.

Syracuse saw the lady of the farm return from town after a couple of hours. Oreo was nowhere to be found. He really didn't know if Oreo was ever coming back home.

He climbed up on the square hay stacked high in the barn. He thought about how Oreo spent every night of the war in this nice, comfortable spot. Syracuse remembered that first night of the war when he had to stay in the cold, dark and dangerous woods while Oreo had this cozy, safe place.

He just hoped he could see young Oreo again. He'd try to fix things.

The next morning the lady of the farm scolded Syracuse for everything that had happened as she served all the cats their breakfast. Feeling guilty he followed her around as she fed the chickens in their coup. She then gave the wild birds both feed to eat and water to drink and bathe in. Syracuse was still by her side. Finally, she refilled the hummingbird feeders with sugar water. He still stayed beside her. He just kept following her.

So she smiled down at Syracuse.

"Old boy, he'll be alright."

She petted him and even got him to wrestle a little bit.

She went back to town later in the morning to bring Oreo back home. Syracuse was waiting on the front porch hoping Oreo would come back with her. As she carried the pet caddy into the house, Syracuse and Oreo looked at each other. Their eyes met for a few seconds.

Oreo would now begin his recuperation stay inside the house.

Even though Oreo was inside, Syracuse wouldn't sleep in that nice area of the barn where Oreo loved to stay. Syracuse decided he'd tough the remaining winter out on top of the vehicle in the carport.

Litter IV

Change on the Old Plot

For eight weeks Oreo stayed inside, recovering from the broken leg his feline war with old Syracuse had caused. It would be mid-March when he finally went back outside.

The day was quite hot for this early spring. However, the weather was getting ready to explode. It would be the first severe weather outbreak of the year.

Being widowed, the lady of the farm was planting some vegetable seeds in the garden all by herself. She was working diligently, knowing the time was right to plant before all the precipitation that would be hear the next few days.

Finally being peaceful with one another, the two tomcats were giving her company wherever she went.

The thunder that was being heard in the background was getting more intense and drawing close. She looked at the storm clouds approaching. So many times she'd experienced this before. She lived in a high tornado risk area. The chance that this could be the storm that does hit her farm was always there. Fascinated, she just stood and stared at the nearing storm. The wind blew harder. It was getting cooler and windy.. Lightning was flashing. Dangerous perhaps, but it was awesome to experience.

You could barely hear it this far away from the town, but the tornado sirens began to roar.

She looked around the property. All the gates were shut well. All the animals were in their pins. The barn was secure. *She always tried to maintain everything*, just in case an emergency *did* happen. And this time she felt glad that she did.

She called for all the cats to come up. Oreo and Syracuse both arrived quickly. Their feud seemed ancient history at this point. She grabbed both of them up and went to the storm cellar in the backyard.

After opening the door, she put the cats on the top steps and made them to go on down. She looked around for Georgette, calling her again and again, but she never came. Out of time, she had to shut the door to the cellar.

Down the steps, now, she turned on a battery operated weather radio and a battery operated camping lantern. She grinned as she noticed her homemade wine bottles fermenting in the cool, dark cellar. Then she decided she'd enjoy a glass of the wine after this storm passed.

The weatherman on the weather radio warned that anybody directly south of the town to get underground immediately. That's exactly where the farm was located.

Outside the wind was blowing the trees so hard. They were half-bent over and shaking violently. The rain was nearly horizontal. Large hail was banging on the top of the cellar on the door. This storm was growing more and more intense.

The old widow just sat back and relaxed. She'd been in the cellar waiting out storms before. At least once or twice a year she would have to sit through a dangerous storm. Living in this area, there is a possible chance that your house *might actually get struck by a tornado.*

After about 30 minutes, the radio said that the storm had left the area. It seemed calm outside, so she decided to venture on out of the cellar. She opened the door and took a wondering look around.

A large tree had fallen on top of the nice hay barn, causing extensive damage. There were tree limbs, both large and small, spread all over the yard. Outdoor furniture had blown over.

She called Georgette's name, but the pussycat never showed herself.

So she went back to the homemade wine she was brewing. She brought it to the house. She grabbed some cheese cloth and strained and filtered the bottle. And then she poured a glass into an old mason jar. She smiled and leaned back in a wooden chair.

It's good to be alive!, she reasoned.

Meanwhile, Georgette was watching the litter of kittens she had just gave birth to only yesterday.\

Litter V
Funk

It sounded like a bird screech. The lady knew what it was, though. Georgette had caught a baby rabbit. As she approached Georgette, the cat turned and ran. The lady scolded her. The cat disappeared into the high grass.

The lady looked at the young rabbit. She instantly knew that it wouldn't make it. She decided to bury the animal. She went just outside the barbwire fence. It separated the yard and the pasture.

There she dug a hole. She placed the young rabbit in it. It was in a plastic bag. The bag was in a shoe box.

Georgette felt guilty. She climbed into the main barn on the property. It had just been partially rebuilt. A tree had fallen on it during the terrible thunderstorm.

Georgette fell asleep. She slept deeply until a noise awoke her. She looked around. It was dark outside. The sound was coming from the main shed. It was near the house.

This was where the food for the cats was placed. It was on a small wooden table. It was too high for any other animals. But the cats could jump up there.

There was a skunk!

Oreo, being a large young tomcat, made his way to the shed. He wanted to encounter this new animal. After all, it was after his food.

The skunk was at the foot of the feeding table. It was just barely high enough that it couldn't make the jump.

Oreo was quietly sneaking up on the skunk.

He got closer….and closer….and closer.

The skunk realized he was there. The skunk sprayed him!

"The name's Funk." The skunk smiled. "It's nice to make your acquaintance?"

Oreo was in shock. The smell was all over him. He could barely even breathe. The smell made him want to vomit. He looked at Funk. The fight was on!

Now Funk could never outrun the much more athletic cat. He didn't have the fighting claws, either. So as Oreo leaped at Funk, carelessly. Funk waited. He had the intent to bite him right when he arrived. Sure enough, Funk bit him right on the nose.

Oreo screamed! It was quite loud. Even the lady in the house woke up. Oreo clawed and bit the skunk. *The skunk sprayed him again.* Oreo was drenched with spray. Still he fought on.

He jumped on top of Funk's back. He nearly bit the skunk's left ear right off.

Funk knew he must retreat. He sprayed a third time. Oreo reacted, turning his head away. Then Funk made a run for it. Oreo decided to not pursue at this point.

Then the lady of the house arrived.

"You're going to get rabies, you dumb cat! That was stupid."

She walked over to her beloved pet. She picked him up. She looked at Oreo's nose. It was bleeding badly.

"I can't believe I have to take you back to the vet, *again*."

Funk made it back to his den safely. He looked at his wife and their six children.

"I didn't get any food….I'm so sorry."

His wife responded, "It sounds like the coyotes are out tonight. You should have them chase you. Run into the farm. Who knows what might happen? We *need* food."

Georgette, had watched everything from high up in one of the barns. She was deeply frightened and worried. She had children, too.

"Where is Syracuse?" She wondered. She loved that old, orange cat.

New Madrid I

The First

It was the morning of December 16, 1811, at 2:15 a.m.

The entire Cole family was in their log cabin in south Missouri, U.S.A. The family had four children, all boys between 5 and 17 years old. The mother's name was Nancy, the father's was Charles.

They were all fast asleep when the massive earthquake struck!

Pans and silverware fell! Guns fell! The home itself crumbled on top of the family! Immediately, the two middle boys of the family were killed! The forest erupted with roars from birds and animals as the ground shook violently!

A few miles away was the nearest other person. He was Homer Thompson. Homer was a retired soldier who'd never really been in any major war. But still he was very skilled in war and survival. Homer was passing through the area hunting a fugitive on the run, named Cletus Cooter.

Homer had built a tent and fire for the night. He was still awake when the earthquake hit. A crack in the ground went right next to Homer! This separated him from his black stallion, which had been tied to a tree. The tree fell over the hole. With the rope around the fallen tree, the stallion was hanging into the crack. It was being hung to death.

Meanwhile, Cletus Cooter fell from the tree he had been hiding in. He hit the ground extremely hard. His forearm was broken.

Cletus was guilty in heart from burning down a schoolhouse of children in a drunken rage. His wife was the teacher. He knew Homer Thompson was tracking him down.

Charles Cole and his wife, battered and bruised, worked frantically through the cold, dark morning! They had managed to get out from under the pile of wood that had been their home for nearly twenty years.

With their children below the rubble, they lifted log after log! Though, they were hurt and freezing, the adrenaline to save their children kept them fighting.

Eventually, Joe and Tom, the 5 year old and the 17 year old, clawed and fought their way out from the pile of logs. The bodies of their brothers remained quiet and motionless.

Homer climbed on top of the fallen tree his horse was hanging from. He managed to cut the rope that was on the top around the tree. The stallion fell and disappeared into the hole in the ground.

He chose to remain where he was at until daylight. He couldn't sleep at all.

As for Cletus, he was hurting badly. He didn't realize it was an earthquake. He reasoned that God was doing something to punish him. He'd done so many wrong things in his life.

Was this "the end" for him?

New Madrid II

Survival

Charles and Nancy Cole didn't have a chance to mourn the death of their two sons. The traveling Homer Thompson didn't get any rest that morning. The fleeing Cletus Cooter wouldn't even pity himself.

It was still Dec. 16, 1811 near the New Madrid Fault. And at 7:15 that morning, a second massive earthquake occurred!

"What's happening?" cried little Joe Cole. "What's happening?"

His father tried to calm him as the world rocked back and forth.

"We'll be O.K., Joe!"

"It'll stop!"

"It'll stop!"

His father was trying not to show himself heartbroken at the lost of his two middle sons. He looked at the rubble that yesterday was the family's cabin. He covered his remaining family tightly, shielding them from the danger of the quake. If anyone else in the family was going to die, it would be him, not his wife or kids!

Homer Thompson was about to finally fall asleep when the second quake began.

The forest rumbled. He looked around. He noticed a few deer running towards him. Then he saw a pack of wild hogs. He was trapped between them and the giant crack in the ground where he was at.

So Homer jumped onto the tree that had fallen across the crack in the ground. He carefully crossed over the moving bridge. However, the animals saw him cross it. Now they were now moving toward him to cross over.

Amidst all the chaos, Homer realized he needed to try shooting some of the game for meat. As always he had kept the gun strapped over his shoulder. The gun was difficult to aim through all the shaking.

A doe and a buck approached the bouncing bridge. As they crossed the tree it finally fell into the abyss below it. The doe went down with it. Homer shot the big buck as it finished its way to his side.

Animals continued to try to jump the crack. Some made it, some didn't.

Meanwhile, Cletus Cooter bravely stood still in the deep forest as the ground shook violently around him. He was in severe pain because of his un-doctored broken wrist from the first quake. He thought to himself this might be the end of his life!

Cletus looked up to the sky! He raised his arms up!

"Almighty God, spare me. Please, spare me!

And the quake coincidentally stopped right then and there!

Cletus smiled in relief. He looked up at the sky as if God had listened to him and rejoiced.

At this point, Cletus could care less that he was a fugitive being tracked down to bring to justice. He was just glad to still be alive.

When the ground finally quit rocking, Charles Cole was just relieved that he hadn't loss anymore children, or his beloved wife. He comforted his young son Joe, who had been so scared by the events.

"See Joe, we're all O.K."

Charles looked at his wife. Then he looked at the crumbled cabin. He looked back at his wife. As their eyes met, they both went to tears for the loss of the two sons that didn't survive the first quake earlier that morning.

Homer Thompson was perplexed. All his essentials, except for his gun and knife, were on the other side of the giant crack in the earth. He had a nice dead buck that he couldn't even clean or cook.

He thought hard. He figured that if the crack had begun from the south, it probably would be shorter across towards its end. Perhaps it would be crossable somewhere. So Homer put the deer over his shoulders and headed north.

Cletus had been fleeing Homer's tracking by heading to the northwest. However, Cletus knew that with no survival skills and a broken wrist, he might actually be better off by allowing Homer to find him. So, Cletus headed south, directly towards Homer Thompson.

Each time a tremor or aftershock occurred, each of these survivors thought to themselves *"Is this divine punishment?"*

Someone Else I

Character Development

Frank Lee-Wright thought that he should try to never think ahead as he wrote his first novel, hoping to keep the product unpredictable. He also had ideas such as writing it in a manner of *extreme detail*. Maybe, *just cover a short time period*? He didn't know.

Still, the first piece of work he was working on was a masterpiece titled WWIII. He knew it had the potential to be a generational book if he could just write it at the level the title was worthy of. However, he had never come near writing such a long book.

Frank, also, suffered from severe mental health problems. He had schizophrenic traits and bipolar disorder *as hard as anyone ever has had.* It had been eleven years since he'd been hospitalized. But previous to that he'd been in and out of institutions every six months, for week long stays, for four or five years. These lockups were during the age of adolescence and young adulthood. Now 34, he could at least manage the situation.

Frank had abused alcohol, marijuana, methamphetamine, and prescription pills as a teenager and young man. He had finally become free of tobacco addiction over ten years ago. He'd only used drugs two times in almost a decade, and it was just pot. He never would overly drink any liquor anymore. He was doing well.

This less self destructive behavior had rewarded him with a nice little apartment and an improved reputation. These were things he never could have had had he still been wasteful with money and committing crimes. He had friends who were now incarcerated. He even had associates who were now dead! He was glad he'd changed.

Frank continued to work on this first novel of his. He pressed on and pressed on. Usually, he would give up on this type of thing. *Not this time!* He actually felt like he was in control of it instead of it being in control of him. It wasn't impossible to finish a novel this go round. The mountain was scalable. Every journey had at last begun with just one step…and then another…and then another!

His plan was to write ten books for two months each over a period of twenty months. *He had some real good writing ideas!* He decided to keep his book ideas to himself. The ideas seemed clever and witty. Frank had already finished a collection of nearly twenty original, quality poems and short works.

In this small town in Oklahoma, U.S.A, Frank was fighting to enjoy his impossible existence. He'd always respond to a person's, "How are you doing?" with his catchphrase, "It's good to be alive!" Sometimes he'd ad even more onto the strange conversation maker, with the words "It's really quite fascinating!"

He simply realized how wonderful life really is. He'd look around with eyes and just soak up life…*impossible and amazing life!!!* Death was his greatest fear. Mortality is a curse that made him angry and scared.

Frank was a very religious person. He dared not fixing the world. Curing the "social problem death"? Fixing equality and happiness for all? He wouldn't. He was taught that you let God handle those matters. Still, he sure was fearful of losing his life, somehow.

He was certainly an obsessive lover of his life. He often wondered just how much his eccentric behavior and comments were having on everybody he'd encountered.

So now this day was coming to a close. Frank had typed on his laptop off and on all day. He'd take a break and watch a ballgame on television. Perhaps, he'd take a little nap. He knew he would have to get more serious if he was to achieve his goals! Watching sports was a major time zapper.

With bedtime now here, Frank saved his novel on both the computer and a flash drive for backup. Afterwards, he checked his e-mails and his bank account's current information. Then he finally turned off his computer for the day.

Frank took the nine pills he normally takes at bedtime for his mental health reasons. Next, he used mouthwash and brushed his teeth. He double checked that the door to his apartment was locked. At last, he climbed onto his bed.

The bed was an open hide-away couch in his bedroom that he never closed back into a couch. It had sheets, a comforter, and pillows. Frank would only sleep on the top of the bed with just a small blanket during the hot summer.

Frank prayed some like he so often does. His main concern was should become a rich and famous writer, instead of living "the normal life". Would it lead to sin? Could he handle being off of a disability check and with free room and board? What if he had to go without all the medicine he takes for his mental survival?

He had experienced being off his meds for just a couple days accidentally on an extended vacation before. He got very, very *desperate and nervous* not being on his medicine.

Within an hour Frank feel asleep easy as he normally does.. This particular night he had an extreme deep sleep. It was like ten hours of death. Frank's alarm went off at 7:30. He usually just got up and reset it for another thirty minutes worth of sleep a few times. But not today!

Frank knew something was wrong. He immediately realized something was different. He could feel that he was now suddenly an elderly man. *He was literally someone else!*

Someone Else II

Geriatric

So *what do you do* when you were 34 years old at bedtime and the next day you magically woke up as an elderly man? You face your mortality!

As Frank awoke, he could hardly move. The body of a 34 year old person and an elderly one was extremely different. He thought about his grandfather. It takes him about 10 seconds to get out of a chair. Then he grabs his cane and uses it to balance himself, as he slowly, slowly moves across the room. *Even with the cane* his balance is shaky. Then he hopes that 30 seconds is enough time to make it to the restroom.

Frank then groaned to himself, thinking about the fact that not only is he old, but he doesn't have the best thing about old age – experience and wisdom.

So Frank very carefully and methodically began to get out of his bed. He knew if he rushed it he might break a bone with a fall. He took an entire minute to sit up on his bed. He could hardly move! He wasn't use to this.

He stopped the alarm clock, that he'd let sound for over a minute. He then made a silent prayer to God to help him with this ordeal. This was serious! This was very serious!

Frank began to search for his shoes. He then realized that his memory wasn't normal anymore, either. He looked around the room. He saw a row of shoes placed neatly, side by side, on the wall on the other side of the bed.

He realized that he would need a walking cane. He decided to lie back down and then work his way across his bed, instead of walking around the room. Lying on his back, he inched and inched, until he was on the other side of the bed. He carefully lowered his feet towards the floor. He painfully leaned over, cautiously, and grabbed the left shoe. He picked up the right shoe, too, since he was already bent over.

It took him a couple of minutes, but he slid the left shoe on, and tied the strings. It took a couple more minutes, and then he finished with the right shoe.

Since he'd only slept on top of the comforter with a small blanket, instead of getting entirely into his bed, he was pretty much already dressed. He just needed to put his shoes on. That was a much needed break for Frank. He sighed, taking a break, but not for very long.

Suddenly, he shuffled his feet, carefully and quick as he could, until he reached the toilet. He'd never had so much trouble using the bathroom. After washing his hands, *he'd spent at over five minutes in that restroom.*

He remembered that he kept his umbrella by the door of the apartment. He thought that it would be the best device as a walking cane at this point. *He would have to physically get to it, though.* He'd use every wall and piece of furniture possible, to brace himself as he went through the apartment. He'd finally make it to the umbrella.

What could he do? Who could he even make a phone call to? Nobody would believe him? This was terrible! He'd never been more terrified and/dumbfounded in his life.

Frank worked his way to his cell phone. He called his mother, whom he was rather close with. Of course, even she didn't believe him. She thought he was joking, intoxicated, or just plain delusional.

Still, he begged her and begged her for help. Finally, she said she'd come over and see him. (She didn't actually believe him, though.)

Frank thought to himself deeply about the reality that he was in. He could die in this condition! He was very old. This was for real! He had to change the complete world in a short period of time! He didn't have a second to waste!

He remembered a line from a poem that he'd actually written himself.

"Give me 'Peace and Security'

So science can concentrate on saving me!"

The Social Problem Death

The young man, a tender 19 year old recently diagnosed with bipolar disorder, climbed out of his bed. There are lithium pills next to him on his nightstand. He's truly the most depressed person in the world. It's 6:00 a.m., five miles from a small town in Oklahoma, the spring of 2000. He makes his way through the old, but nice, little house on what hasn't been sold away of his grandmother's 70 acres. He looks in the vanity mirror by the bathroom. He's covered with acne. He's not chiseled physique-wise. He looks terrible.

He just doesn't understand how life can be this way. How can a mental health problem do so much damage? How can it make a person this unhappy, this disabled?

He thinks back to just less than three years ago. He'd been considered the best looking guy in his high school. He was the ultimate ladies man. Though raised poor, he was raised right. He had a lot going for him. He had dated many beautiful young ladies. He was cool. He was respected. He was successful. Now what? The worse possible scenario!

He painfully heads back to bed, instead of going to the local community college where he is enrolled. He'd made it to be a sophomore in college. This was due to gaining a GED and making great grades, on his second chance in life, which was that collegiate freshman year. He'd fought back.

But now, about 10:00 a.m., he does finally crawl out of bed, but begins to play video games rebelliously to those who think he should be a better person. He's suicidal. Life is in complete despair.

At 11:00 he arrives for one of the several classes in school he's now failing in. *He hears things in what people say that others don't hear. He sees games to play with body language that others don't see.* He looks so depressed. He is now *such* a loser. He walks out of the class in less than ten minutes.

That afternoon, he drives to the local mental health office for a 1:00 appointment. Even there, he is delusional. *He hears the radio playing, but thinks every song is for him, and that there are cameras and satellite feeds watching him, showing him to the DJs, not to mention Hollywood and the Government.* They tell him he's delusional. He can't avoid hearing the insanity, though.

He now heads to work. The restaurant in town that he works at that tries to understand his mental health. Still, he's the dishwasher, 2:00 to 10:00, Monday through Friday. He often gets angry and leaves in a few hours. He rarely makes it through his entire shift.

Once he gets there, he enters the building and goes to his spot. They have all the dishes from lunch that day waiting on him. He stays several hours this day. However, he was outright insane. *He played games on how to stack bowls, plates, and silverware. He mimics noises with others, thinking it is normal, which it isn't. The radio plays and the songs depress him. Actually, he thinks that there is a camera in the ceiling vent above him that feeds into the DJ's studio.*

Finally, he runs out mad!

He gets home and everyone is mad as him for doing what he did. He just looks forward to Monday Night Football.

He spends the whole game thinking they see him in the booth through satellite feed. What hurt him the most during all this is that *the voices he hears are not nice and friendly. They are mean and hurtful.*

Bedtime arrives. He smokes one last cigarette. He lies down to sleep. *He fights the desire to mimic noises within that house and the satellite feeds.*

Suicide can happen.

www.ingramcontent.com/pod-product-compliance
Lightning Source LLC
Chambersburg PA
CBHW081022040426
42444CB00014B/3320